The Redouté Album

ACKNOWLEDGEMENTS

The authors and publishers would like to thank The Royal Horticultural Society, London: the Lindley Librarian, Brent Elliott and his staff for their help in the compilation of this book.

They would also like to thank the following for their kind permission to photograph the original prints in their possession: The Royal Horticultural Society for the plates appearing on pages 9, 11, 13, 15, 17, 19, 21, 23, 25, 27, 29, 31, 33, 35, 37, 39, 41, 43, 45, 47, 49, 51, 53, 55, 57, 59, 61, 63, 65, 67, 69, 71, 73, 75, 77, 79, 81, 83, 87, 91, 93, 95, 97, 99, 101, 103, 105, 107, 109, 111, 113, 115, 117, 119, 121, 123 and 127. The Fitzwilliam Museum, Cambridge for the plates appearing on pages 85, 89 and 125.

The Redouté Album
This edition published in the USA by Dorset Press, 1990
Dorset Press is a division of Marboro Book Corporation

Copyright © Studio Editions Ltd., 1990
Princess House, 50 Eastcastle Street
London W1N 7AP, England.

Printed and bound in Hong Kong

ISBN 0-88029-575-9

The Redouté Album

Pois de senteur.   Lathyrus odoratus.

P. J. Redouté.   Langlois.

Martyn and Alison Rix

DORSET PRESS
NEW YORK

CONTENTS

INTRODUCTION

Few botanical painters have achieved the world-wide recognition accorded to Pierre-Joseph Redouté; reproductions of his paintings, especially of roses, today adorn the rooms of houses great and small, in the form of paintings, original and reproduction prints, table-mats, wastepaper-baskets, tea-trays and all manner of other objects. He was even fortunate enough to have been recognized as a great artist in his own lifetime, although he was so feckless with money that he was later forced to turn out more and more paintings to support the style of life to which he had become accustomed. While these added greatly to the sheer volume of his work, their quality did not always match his earlier high standards.

Redouté's working life coincided with the last years of the old monarchy in France, and continued through the Revolution to the time of Napoleon and the second restoration of the monarchy under Louis Phillipe. At the beginning of his career he worked for Marie-Antoinette, and in spite of this, survived the Reign of Terror, and reached the peak of his artistic and scientific output under the patronage of Napoleon's first wife, the Empress Joséphine.

In no country other than France could a flower painter have achieved such prominence and success. There were equally talented and accomplished flower painters working in England at the same time, but none of them have become nearly as well known as Redouté. For Redouté's life was the culmination of a long tradition of Royal patronage of botanical painting that went back over two hundred years to the Renaissance in Italy.

During classical and medieval times most medicines were derived from plants, and botany was considered a branch of medicine. Botanical paintings were used to illustrate herbals, and were usually very crude engravings copied from one book to the next. At the same time, flowers were used as decorations in other paintings or in the borders of devotional manuscripts. Albrecht Dürer was one of the first painters whose detailed flower paintings have survived. They are sufficiently complete to show that they were not mere studies to be used elsewhere in more important paintings. A very fine example of Dürer's work is a *gouache* of paeonies which dates from around 1503, but flower painting was only a very minor part of his amazingly varied output. Dürer's dictum, perhaps to his pupil, the botanical painter Hans Weiditz, has often been repeated, but not bettered: "Study nature diligently, be guided by nature and do not depart from it, thinking that you can do better yourself; you will surely be misguided, for truly art is hidden in nature, and he who can draw it out, possesses it."

The first botanical illustrator whose works have survived in significant numbers is the Italian Jacopo Ligozzi. He was born in Verona in 1547, and arrived in Florence in around 1577, where he became court painter to the Grand Duke of Tuscany, Francesco de Medici, and later, superintendent of the Uffizi Gallery, where many of his flower paintings can still be seen. As well as flowers, Ligozzi painted birds and animals, and designed theatre sets, costumes and classical scenes and swags, possibly for tapestries, or for decorative panels. His flower paintings, however, were his great triumph, done in watercolour and *gouache*, and both botanically accurate and artistic, so that they stand comparison with the best work of the eighteenth century. Ligozzi was associated with the botanist Aldovandrus, who founded, in Bologna one of the first botanic gardens: his paintings include both native Italian plants and new introductions from Mexico, tropical Africa or the Levant, then under the civilized influence of the Ottoman Turks, themselves great flower lovers and gardeners.

The tradition of Royal patronage for flower painting was brought to France from Florence in the early seventeenth century by Marie de Medici who was married to Henri IV in 1600, and became Regent of France after his assassination in 1610. *Le Jardin du roy très Chrestien Henry IV, Roy de France and de Navare, dédié à la Reyne*, was published in 1608, by Pierre Vallet; it was intended as a pattern book for embroidery. From Vallet onwards there was always a botanical painter at the French court. Vallet's successor was Daniel Rabel (1579–1637), who combined great talent in flower painting with portraiture, landscape painting and designs for the ballet; one of his more unusual commissions was his dispatch by Marie de Medici to the Spanish court to paint a portrait of Anne of Austria, fiancée of Louis XIII.

Without doubt, the greatest of the flower painters of the seventeenth century was Nicholas Robert. It was his paintings of flowers, birds and animals done for Gaston d'Orléans, brother of Louis XIII, which formed the basis of the royal collection of *vélins* (so called because they were painted on vellum), to which Redouté was to contribute over five hundred fine paintings. Robert's masterpiece was the huge *Recueil des Fleurs*, with most of the plates both drawn and engraved by Robert himself. The plates were published on their own in 1701, but the complete work did not appear until 1788, when it was entitled *Mémoires pour servir à l'histoire des plantes*. In size and style it is reminiscent of Redouté's *Geraniologia* which appeared about three years later, but Robert's use of cross-hatching for shading is cruder than the pure line used by Redouté's engravers.

Robert was followed by the little-known Jean Joubert who continued to add to the *vélins*, but did not illustrate any published work; he did however discover and train the young

Claude Aubriet, who accompanied Joseph Pitton de Tournefort on his important journey to the Levant, travelling as far east as Erzurum and Tiflis in Armenia, and climbing onto Mount Ararat, which they found very dry and dusty, and where they were alarmed to see two tigers. The results of this journey were published in *Relation d'un Voyage au Levant* (1718), and in Jaubert and Spach's *Illustrationes plantarum Orientalum* (1842–1857).

Between the death of Aubriet in 1742 and Redouté's arrival in Paris in 1782, the position of Royal Botanical Draughtsman and Professor of Flower Painting was held first by Madeleine Basseporte, then by Gérard van Spaëndonck (1746–1822). It was van Spaëndonck who was Redouté's teacher, and whose technical discoveries, according to Wilfred Blunt, Redouté exploited and popularized. Before van Spaëndonck, French botanical paintings were artistic and accurate or even, as in the case of Robert, splendid. Van Spaëndonck, a follower of the Dutch painter Jan van Huysum (1682–1749), introduced to France a voluptuousness and richness which can also be seen in Redouté's mature work. Redouté had also studied van Huysum's work in Amsterdam, and his delight in double roses and paeonies and in veined and puckered leaves, can be seen in many paintings, notably that of the lettuce-leaved rose, *Rosa Centifolia Bullata*. Before van Spaëndonck's arrival in Paris, the *vélins* were painted in *gouache*, an opaque watercolour, and his own earliest *vélins* are in *gouache* too, but around 1783 he began to use pure watercolour, and the *vélins* painted after 1784 are watercolours of the greatest skill and beauty, equal to the finest painted by Redouté himself.

Redouté's own style was influenced by his association with L'Héritier, for whom he produced the majority of the plates in *Stirpes novae*, and this early training in botanical accuracy and the dissection of the parts of flowers was most important for his development as a botanical illustrator.

While visiting London with L'Héritier, in circumstances described later, he met the botanists and botanical artists who congregated at Sir Joseph Banks's house, and from them he learnt some of the new colour printing techniques that he was later to develop so successfully. Of particular interest to him was the work of the prolific engraver Francesco Bartolozzi (1727–1815), who had developed the technique of stipple engraving, which involves the use of variously spaced dots, rather than lines, as previously. This technique, when carried out by a skilful engraver, is extremely subtle and produces a much more delicate effect than line engraving.

In the technique of line engraving, then well established, fine lines are engraved in a copper plate, which is then inked, the surplus ink cleaned off, and the print made from the ink trapped in the grooves. In the earlier books to which Redouté contributed, the plates were printed in black, and could have been hand-coloured; later ones were printed in green ink for stems and leaves, brown for roots, and lesser colours were applied by hand. An example of this is the plate of *Cornus canadensis* (Page 11), published in 1788.

On his return from London in 1877, Redouté was invited to contribute to the *vélins* by van Spaëndonck, who had also been experimenting with stipple as a means of reproducing the delicate shading on the petals of flowers such as irises. In stipple engraving the image is engraved in fine dots, thinly distributed on the highlights, densely in the shadows. Van Spaëndonck and Redouté developed a colour printed stipple, in which the plates were painted with coloured inks before being printed, so that a colour print was obtained. These prints were then retouched by hand, and any very small colour

details added. This coloured stipple was first used in *Plantes Grasses* published in parts between 1799 and 1831, with text by de Candolle.

During their earlier years in Paris, Redouté and his younger brother Henri-Joseph were taken onto the staff of the Natural History Museum. Here they illustrated a number of purely scientific botanical books, such as Desfontaines *Flora Atlantica* (1798–1800), and De Candolle's monograph of *Astragalus* (1802), both issued only in black and white, in a combination of line and stipple engraving. Though generally less lavish than those produced before the Revolution, these black and white plates were among the finest engravings ever made of plants.

Redouté was succeeded in this type of work by a number of younger painters, notably his pupil Pancrace Bessa (1772–1835); Bessa worked with Redouté on many of his more scientific works, and even signed himself, Élève de Redouté. The later volumes of the monumental second edition of *Traité des Arbres et Arbustes* by Duhamel de Monceau were almost entirely illustrated by Bessa, who also made significant contributions to Michaux's *North American Sylva*, and other books usually associated with Redouté.

Henri-Joseph Redouté (1766–1852) specialized in fish and reptiles, but also produced a large number of flower paintings, and it is often not possible to detect, apart from the signature, any difference between the brothers' work. Henri-Joseph accompanied Napoleon on his Egyptian campaign, and there contracted an eye disease which shortened his working life.

Pierre Jean François Turpin (1775–1840), and Antoine Poiteau (1766–1854), are often linked because they were friends and collaborated on numerous important botanical works, particularly on South American plants. Turpin was primarily a painter, Poiteau a botanist; their most important collaboration was with the great German naturalist, Alexander von Humboldt, on his *Plantes Equinoxiales*, and *Monographie des Melastomacese*, the orginals of which are in the Fitzwilliam Museum, Cambridge. Their drawings appeared with Redouté's in books such as La Billardière's *Icones Plantarum Syriae Rariorum* (1791–1812).

Apart from Redouté's scientific pupils, there were a number of young ladies to whom he gave lessons in flower painting, to while away, as Wilfrid Blunt says, the aimless years between adolescence and matrimony. Many of them exhibited at the Salon in Paris in the 1830's and 1840's, and their work is often accomplished but usually in Redouté's style.

Alfred Riocreux (1820–1912), by his long life, brings Redouté's style and tradition into the twentieth century. His engraved work shows great accuracy and perfect elegance, but he never achieved any of Redouté's popular success. He spent his life, as far as one can tell, working in the Natural History Museum in Paris, drawing the plants, including algae and fungi, brought back by expeditions to distant parts of the world. Some of his earliest work was for Victor Jacquemont's posthumous *Voyage dans l'Inde* published in 1841. Some of his later work in the 1870's is reproduced by lithography, a process invented in 1797, in which the artist draws in waxed pencil on dry porous limestone. When the stone is wetted, the printer's oily ink adheres only to the waxed area. This allows great freedom of line and delicacy of shading, ideal for illustrations intended to be hand-coloured. Lithography, now generally using zinc plates instead of stone, is a much quicker technique than engraving, which declined for this reason, and most plant illustrations from the mid-nineteenth century onwards were lithographed rather than engraved.

CHAPTER I

PIERRE-JOSEPH REDOUTÉ:
HIS EARLY LIFE

Pierre-Joseph Redouté was born in 1759 in the small town of St-Hubert in the Belgian Ardennes, where his father, Charles-Joseph (1715–1776) was employed as a painter and decorator in the ancient Abbey. The Redoutés had five children, of whom three, Antoine-Ferdinand, Pierre-Joseph and Henri-Joseph, showed promise as painters. The family had a tradition of working as artists and craftsmen throughout Belgium, and each generation handed down their skills to the next. Charles-Joseph had himself been taught by his father, and at a young age had gone off to Paris in search of work, stopping to work in the studios of various master painters on the way. To Charles-Joseph, Paris was the artist's mecca; he had been a student at the Academy of Saint-Luc, paying for his tuition by painting portraits and scenes of classical or biblical subjects. After a while he had returned to Belgium and was commissioned to beautify the Abbey and Basilica in a suitably lavish style by the Lord Abbot of St Hubert, a monk who had previously spent much time at the court of Louis XV and thus had a great knowledge of the marvellous works of art at Versailles.

Pierre-Joseph was therefore brought up in a humble home, but with access to inspiring buildings and paintings, a combination which helped to shape his later career. He was fortunate as a boy to be befriended by one of his teachers, a monk at the Abbey, who was a keen naturalist and herbalist. Redouté often accompanied this man on his trips into the local woods and meadows, where they searched for the herbs and medicinal plants needed for the Abbey pharmacy; in this way, Redouté learnt to recognize the wild plants and to know something of their medicinal properties. Here too he would have had the opportunity to see some of the illustrated herbals that the monks had in their library.

In 1772, at the age of thirteen, Redouté left home to work as an itinerant painter and decorator. He produced portraits for merchants and other well-to-do people, biblical scenes for village churches, and played a part in decorating a number of fine houses; he visited Amsterdam, to study the work of the great Dutch masters, in particular Jan van Huysum, who specialized in large, flamboyant flower pieces. From this time, Redouté began to sketch flowers at every opportunity, and to include flowers in his portraits and other paintings. On his return to Belgium he was commissioned to decorate part of the Château de Carlsbourg, and here he was able to give full rein to his desire to paint flowers. Once this commission came to an end, he worked his way to Liège, where he studied with the Cocklers, a family of painters well-known in their day, and through them he obtained work in Luxembourg, where he painted portraits. One of these was for an enthusiastic patron of the arts, the Princesse-Baronne de Tornaco, who in turn encouraged him to go to Paris, and furnished him with letters of introduction to a number of high-ranking patrons of the arts. Shortly after this, Redouté was invited by his elder brother, Antoine-Ferdinand, to come to Paris to assist him in his current job of decorating a new theatre. Once there, he worked on the theatre during the day, and spent his spare time painting flowers. He was fortunate that the Jardin du Roi (now the Jardin des Plantes) was near his lodgings, and here he was able to spend many hours sketching plants. It was here also that he made the acquaintance of an art dealer, who commissioned him to paint a number of flowers, which were then engraved by the Belgian, de Marteau, and published as models for students interested in flower painting. Redouté took this opportunity of learning the process of engraving and colour printing (from de Marteau).

In 1876, Redouté married Marie-Marthe Gobert, a French girl who bore him two daughters, and who seems to have proved herself a loyal, tolerant and loving wife; little is known of her, except that after his death, when she was short of money, she published a slim volume entitled *Le Bouquet Royale*, containing five plates drawn and engraved by Redouté.

Redouté continued to paint in the Jardin du Roi, which was both a botanic garden and a centre for the study of natural history, and it was there that he met the botanist, Charles-Louis L'Héritier de Brutelle, who engaged him as a botanical artist, to illustrate a new book which he was planning to publish. This partnership was to prove a turning point in Redouté's life, for not only did L'Héritier provide him with a regular income, but he also took him under his wing and taught him the basics of botany. In L'Héritier's two gardens, in Paris and Picardy, he grew all the newest and most interesting plants which were at that time flooding into Europe as a result of the labours of great plant collectors such as Dombey in South America. This meant that Redouté always had access to new and different plants to paint, and in fact this was the main purpose of his work for L'Héritier, as the book on which he was engaged was titled *Stirpes novae aut minus cognitae*. Redouté produced fifty-four of the ninety-one illustrations in *Stirpes novae*, and they appear to be his earliest published drawings. In comparison with his later work they are somewhat stiff, although this may be partly due to the quality of the engraving, which in this case uses entirely lines, rather than the stipple he used later. Some of the copies were only printed in black, although a number were hand-coloured.

STIRPES NOVAE AUT MINUS COGNITAE, *quas descriptionibus et iconibus illustravit.* New or less-known plants, which are illustrated by descriptions and pictures, was published in six parts, from 1784–1791. The text for this work was written by Charles Louis L'Héritier de Brutelle, the botanist who taught Redouté how to make accurate and detailed drawings of plants. Redouté contributed fifty-four of the ninety-one colour plates, and a number of unpublished paintings (the project was never completed due to L'Héritier's reduced circumstances after the Revolution) are in the possession of the Lindley Library, London.

Solanum cornutum L.

This annual plant is a native of Mexico, and requires warmth and greenhouse protection to grow well in Britain; the name 'cornutum' refers to the single long, curved, horn-like stamen. The majority of solanums are found in South America (although the aubergine, S. *melongena*, is native to Africa and southern Asia), and it is from here that the most familiar garden solanums, such as the potato, S. *tuberosum*, originated. *Solanum capsicastrum*, the winter cherry, is popular as an annual houseplant, while S. *crispum* and the less hardy S. *jasminoides* can be grown as climbers outside in mild parts of Britain, and southern and western North America.

Cornus. *Specimen botanicum sistens descriptiones et icones specierum Corni minus cognitarum.* A botanical specimen, consisting of descriptions and pictures of less-known species of dogwood is a slim volume, with fifteen pages and six colour plates, published in 1788. Another collaboration between L'Héritier, Freret (who contributed many plates to *Stirpes novae*) and Redouté, this little book employs the technique of line engraving, which gives a very clear image in contrast to the rather delicate but vague effect of the stipple used by Redouté in later works. Coloured plates for this book were printed in green, while black ink was used for black and white versions of the same plates.

Cornus canadensis L.

The dwarf cornel is a herbaceous plant, native to North America, Japan and Siberia, where it grows in peaty bogs and coniferous woods, creeping by underground stems through the moss. The heads of minute flowers, surrounded by petal-like bracts, appear in May to July, and sometimes red berries are produced in the autumn. It is much easier to grow than the very similar, black-berried *Cornus suecica*, with which it is often confused, and in gardens associates happily with heathers or other peat-loving plants.

P. J. Redouté del.

Devisse sculp.

C O R N U S canadensis. *L.*

CHAPTER II

THE REVOLUTION: 1789–1798

It is hard to remember today that Redouté's early life in Paris was lived against the backdrop of the violence and social upheaval of the Revolution. Most of his work was for aristocratic patrons, and suited the tastes of the book-buying educated classes, and yet it appears that he was never short of work or really materially affected at all by the events which surrounded him. Though L'Héritier was imprisoned and had a near escape from the guillotine in the days of the Terror, he was saved, possibly due to his credentials as a man of the utmost integrity and fairness; (he served as a magistrate in the influential *Cour des Aides*, which specialized in obtaining fair taxes for ordinary people). He did however lose a great deal of money during the Revolution, with the result that *Stirpes novae*, which was published in instalments, was never completed. A number of unpublished aquatints originally prepared for this work are now in the Lindley Library of The Royal Horticultural Society, London, and some of these, such as *Michauxia campanuloides*, were later issued as 'Monographies'.

Redouté collaborated with L'Héritier on two other books which were published in 1788: *Geraniologia*, with forty-four engravings, thirty-three of which were contributed by Redouté, one by his brother, Henri-Joseph, and the rest by other artists; and *Cornus*, a slim volume containing six colour plates by Redouté and Freret. In the autumn of 1788, L'Héritier undertook an extraordinary trip to England. The reason for this was that the herbarium assembled from an expedition to Peru and Chile by Joseph Dombey, a young French plant hunter, was the subject of a disagreement between the French and Spanish Governments, the joint sponsors of the trip. The collection had been divided between the two countries in South America, and placed on two separate ships;

Plantarum succulentarum Historia; *Histoire Naturelle des Plantes Grasses, avec leurs figures en couleurs*. The Natural History of Fleshy Plants, with their pictures in colour was published in Paris in thirty-one parts, from 1799–1831. It is the first book illustrated entirely by Redouté, who painted and engraved 188 colour plates, using his new stipple method. It is the only book for which Redouté engraved all the plates himself, and it is also interesting that it is the first publication in which he left out the traditional frame around the flowers; he never seems to have returned to this conventional way of presenting a botanical painting. The text was written by Augustin Pyramus de Candolle (1778–1841), a Swiss botanist whose chief claim to fame was the natural system of plant classification which he devised and published in his *Théorie Elementaire de la Botanique* (1813).

Aloe variegata L.

This aloe, sometimes known as the partridge-breasted aloe on account of the V-shaped markings which are similar to those on the breast of the Common or English partridge, is a native of Cape Province in South Africa, where it grows in partial shade on stony ground. It is a small plant with stiff, hard leaves, and, being very drought-resistant and tolerant of neglect, has long been grown on cottage window-sills.

ALOE variegata.   ALOÈS panaché.

the Spanish ship had subsequently been lost at sea, with the result that the remaining collection had been impounded by the Spanish. After much wrangling, during which virtually all the living plants had died, the Spanish authorities finally gave Dombey permission to take his share of what remained of the herbarium specimens. Poor Dombey had then discovered that the French Government were not inclined to take any interest in the hard-won collection at all, let alone pay for the cost of housing it nor publish details. L'Héritier stepped in and offered to publish the results of the expedition himself. Imagine his fury, then, when, a short time later, the Spanish Government decided to object in the strongest possible terms to the publication of the work in France, and demanded the return of the specimens forthwith. The French Government were not inclined to incur

the displeasure of the Spaniards, and probably would have agreed to their demands, but L'Héritier took the matter into his own hands, and with Redouté's help, packed and removed the collection to Sir Joseph Banks's house in London.

Sir Joseph Banks (1744–1820) was renowned as a botanist and explorer (he had visited Newfoundland and Iceland in search of plants, and later sailed round the world with Captain Cook) and was most hospitable to all who were interested in the study of natural history. L'Héritier was given the run of his fine library and herbarium, and so enjoyed his time in London, and in particular his visits to Kew Gardens, that he not only extended his visit to well over a year, but also invited Redouté to join him. L'Héritier took the opportunity to study many of the new and rare plants that were being grown in England, and

Cactus grandiflorus L.

This exotic cactus, now correctly called *Selenicereus grandiflorus* Britton & Rose, or Queen of the Night, is so called because the flowers open at dusk and are fading by morning; (*Selene* is the Greek for moon). It is a native of Jamaica and Cuba, where it grows by scrambling over trees and rocks.

It grows easily, but does not flower freely in cultivation. This may be the species which Redouté was summoned to the Temple to paint for the imprisoned Marie-Antoinette, in the middle of the night.

CACTUS grandiflorus.   CIERGE à grande fleur.

P. J. Redouté, del.

after a while decided to publish an illustrated account of some of them, as a compliment to his hosts. He engaged James Sowerby, who later achieved prominence for his *English Botany*, and started work on the new project which was entitled *Sertum Anglicum seu Plantae Rariores quae in hortis juxta Londinium, imprimis in horto regio Kewensis excoluntur ab anno 1786 ad annum 1787 observatae*, or *Sertum Anglicum* for short! The resulting book contained twenty-two plates by Redouté and thirteen by Sowerby, with a dedication to the English Nation, in gratitude for their kindness and hospitality. The text was published first, in 1788, the plates afterwards; all the plates are line engravings, from monochrome paintings by the two artists, and as far as is known, no coloured copies exist.

Redouté also worked on Dombey's South American collections, and there is a group of five monochrome paintings by him in the Fitzwilliam Museum, Cambridge, done in 1786 and 1787. These include *Desfontainea spinosa*, a native of Chile and Peru, which is not recorded in cultivation in England until 1843.

On his return to Paris, in December 1787, Redouté made the acquaintance of another friend of L'Héritier, Gérard van Spaëndonck, a Dutch artist who had arrived in Paris in 1766. He had been a fashionable painter of snuff boxes and flower pieces in the grand manner of van Huysum prior to becoming Professeur de Peinture de Fleurs at the Jardin du Roi in 1780; one of his responsibilities was to add to the royal collection of *vélins*, which had been begun by Jean Baptiste Gaston, Duc d'Orléans (1608–1660), brother of Louis XIII, during his exile at Blois, on the Loire. Gaston had engaged the most gifted artists of the time to paint the animals and birds in his menagerie, and the most rare and beautiful flowers in his garden at Blois, and on his death he left the resulting collection of *gouache* paintings on vellum to

Cactus mamillaris L.

This cactus, and related species are now put in a separate genus *Mamillaria*, referring to the nipple-like projections on which the rosettes of bristles sit, that are characteristic of most cactuses.

Cactus mamillaris is now called *Mamillaria mamillaris*, and is a native of Venezuela and nearby islands in the West Indies. Most *Mamillaria* species are easy to grow, and make attractive dwarf specimens in a greenhouse or on a sunny window-sill. One species, *Mamillaria vivipara*, is a native of western North America, from Manitoba and Alberta southwards to Kansas and Colorado, so it may be expected to survive intense cold in winter, provided it is kept very dry.

his nephew, King Louis XIV. The collection remained in the hands of the Royal Family at Versailles, and was continually enlarged by the best artists of the day. Van Spaëndonck himself painted a number of *gouaches* for the *vélins* during the years 1780–1782, but by 1784 he had changed to watercolour, a practice which was followed by Redouté when he was commissioned by van Spaëndonck to contribute to the *vélins*. These early paintings were left unsigned, as were those by artists other than van Spaëndonck himself.

By this time, Redouté's work was beginning to become well-known, and in 1877 he was appointed flower painter to Queen Marie-Antoinette (1755–1793); the post does not seem to have involved teaching the Queen how to paint, but rather to record her favourite plants in the garden of the Pétit Trianon, the idyllic and extravagant playground where she managed to ignore the growing discontent of the French people. The subsequent story of the Royal family's attempt to flee the country, the storming of the Tuileries, and the family's incarceration in the Temple are only too well-known, but there is one incident that may not be quite so familiar; it seems that the Queen was allowed to keep a night-flowering cactus, of which she was particularly fond, with her in prison, and one day Redouté was commanded to present himself at the Temple that night in order that he might paint the cactus flower as it opened. The pathetic queen was executed soon afterwards (August 1793), and there seems to be no record of what happened to the painting. On the death of the Royal Family, the *vélins* were declared the property of the state and were taken to the Muséum National D'Histoire Naturelle (the new name for the Jardin du Roi), where Redouté and his younger brother Henri-Joseph (who specialized in painting animals) continued to add to the collection.

Cotyledon orbiculata L.

This succulent plant is a member of the *Crassula* family. It is a native of southern Africa from the Cape northwards to the Limpopo river, where it forms a small shrub or clump of short stems to three feet tall, but usually less, and grows on cliffs, in dry rocky places and in scrub. The variety *oblonga* (Haw.) DC., is found at nearly nine thousand feet in the Drakensberg mountains, and can survive several degrees of frost, provided that it is dry. Redouté's painting does not really do justice to this plant, which can have shining white leaves and large heads of orange flowers. It is easily grown in very well-drained soil.

COTYLEDON orbiculata.   COTYLEDON orbiculaire.

P. J. Redouté pinx.

Pelargonium tetragonum (L. FIL.) L'HÉRITIER

Of the 250 or so species of *Pelargonium* known to science, over half are found in the Cape region of South Africa, and it is from there that all the parents of the modern geraniums, as they are commonly called, originated. *Pelargonium tetragonum* is found in semi-desert areas in the Cape, east to Grahamstown, and inland on the edge of the Karoo. It grows in scrub and on dry rocky hills, forming a succulent bush up to six feet high, with bluntly four-angled stems, hence the specific name. The flowers have two large upper petals about two inches long, and may be cream or pale pink.

L'Héritier was the author of a monograph on geraniums, pelargoniums and related genera, published in 1791–1792, and thirty-three of the forty-four plates were done by Redouté. They are large, fine engravings, but were only issued in black and white, and the text was never published, L'Héritier's names being taken up by other authors.

PELARGONIUM tetragonum.　　PÉLARGONE tétragone.

J.P. Redouté pinx.

CHAPTER III

ASSOCIATION WITH THE EMPRESS JOSÉPHINE

But for the death of Robespierre, mastermind of the Reign of Terror which gripped Paris during the years 1793–1794, it is unlikely that Joséphine would have lived to become one of the greatest patrons of the arts in France. Born Marie-Joséphine-Rose Tascher de la Pagerie in the West Indies in 1763, she came to France and married the Vicomte de Beauharnais by whom she had two children. Although the couple were later legally separated, their aristocratic status meant that they were both imprisoned during the Reign of Terror, and Beauharnais was executed in 1794. It seems certain that Joséphine would have suffered the same fate, but fortunately the tide of public opinion turned against Robespierre, who by this time had become virtual dictator of France, and on July 28, 1794 he was himself sent to the guillotine. Joséphine and hundreds of other prisoners were freed, and in March 1796, two days before his departure for Italy, she married Napoleon Bonaparte, who had just been appointed commander of the army there. In 1799, by which time Napoleon had proved himself to be a ruthless and successful soldier and become First Consul of France under the new constitution, Joséphine acquired the estate of Malmaison near Paris, and here she indulged her love of flowers and animals.

1799 was an auspicious year for Redouté, as it saw the successful publication of the first instalment of his *Plantarum succulentarum Historia*, or *Histoire Naturelle des Plantes Grasses*, the idea for which had been suggested to him by L'Héritier, who pointed out that it was impossible to make herbarium specimens of succulent plants and that therefore it would be invaluable to botanists to have detailed and accurate drawings and descriptions of them drawn from living specimens. By this time, L'Héritier's wealth was

LES LILIACÉES. The eight folio volumes published in parts by Redouté between 1802 and 1816, is considered by many to be the finest, though perhaps not best known, of all his works. Every one of the 486 plates was painted by Redouté himself, colour printed from engraved plates, and then 'finished' by hand by one of Redouté's assistants; in addition, eighteen sets on large paper were hand finished by Redouté himself. The text for the first four volumes was written by Augustin Pyramus de Candolle; that accompanying the next two volumes was contributed by François Delaroche, and Alire Raffeneau-Delile dealt with Volume VIII. *Les Liliacées* contains not only paintings of true lilies, and related plants such as fritillaries and erythroniums, but also members of other families such as *Iris* and *Amaryllis*. An interesting minor detail is that the original paintings for most of the first thirty plates retain their frames (see pages 89 and 91), but these were omitted during the engraving process.

Dianella ensifolia (L.) REDOUTÉ

This species is sometimes known under the name *Dianella nemorosa* Lam.; it is a native of tropical parts of Asia, from Java northwards to Japan, on the coast of Honshu. The hardier species of *Dianella* are native to Australia and New Zealand, where they grow in woods, and shady places, and they require shade and shelter in cultivation. Though the flowers are small, the leaves are very elegant, and the blue or purple berries are most unusual.

considerably reduced, and he was unable to publish botanical books as he had done previously, but he never lost his enthusiasm for new projects of this kind. It was one of L'Héritier's friends, Desfontaines, who introduced Redouté to both a publisher, M. Garnery, who was prepared to publish the work in fifty instalments, and Augustin Pyramus de Candolle, a young Swiss botanist, who undertook to write the accompanying text. Fired by the success of *Plantes Grasses*, Redouté decided to start making drawings and paintings of the lily family, with a view to publishing, at his own expense, a similar work illustrating this group of plants which were as beautiful in life as they were unattractive in the herbarium. By this time, Redouté was earning a comfortable living by illustrating botanical books, and he also received a regular salary for his work in the Museum along with free accommodation in the former Royal Palace of the Louvre. He had, again through L'Hér-itier, met Jacques-Martin Cels, who had a famous garden stocked with unusual plants in Paris, and through him had made the acquaintance of the botanist, Étienne-Pierre Ventenat who was describing many of the plants growing in Cels's garden. Redouté contributed the illustrations to the resulting *Description des Plantes nouvelles et peu connues, cultivées dans le Jardin de J.M. Cels*, which was published in 1800, and by 1803 the trio had produced a further selection, entitled *Choix des Plantes, donc la plupart sont cultivées dans le Jardin de Cels*, which included paintings by Bessa, Turpin, Poiteau, and Henri-Joseph Redouté as well. This association with Ventenat produced another bonus for Redouté, when Ventenat was appointed the official botanist of Malmaison, and Redouté was asked to paint the flowers in Joséphine's garden. So began a long and fruitful association and friendship, which lasted until Joséphine's death.

Asparagus tenuifolius Lam.

This species is native to southern Europe, parts of Russia and of north-western Turkey. It is usually found in woods, in the mountains, and in rather dry meadows. It differs from the common asparagus in the arrangement of the fine leaf-like cladodes which are grouped in bunches, a long-stalked flower hanging from each.

The common asparagus, (*Asparagus officinalis*), so much esteemed as a vegetable, is native to most of Europe except the far north, eastwards to Central Asia, and usually grows wild in rather dry sandy places, on coastal dunes, deserts and steppes. I have eaten a fair dish of rather thin shoots, which were growing in quantity on the dusty volcanic slopes of Mount Ararat.

Asparagus Tenuifolius.   *Asperge à feuilles menues.*

When Joséphine first moved into Malmaison the house was thoroughly dilapidated, and the gardens had been neglected. However, Joséphine, a woman of determination and charm, set to work and with great effort, and considerable expenditure, managed to turn the estate into a delightful refuge for herself and Napoleon, on the rare occasions that he was on leave. By a strange coincidence, one of the first painter-decorators to work on the house was Antoine-Ferdinand, Redouté's brother. Joséphine soon came to love plants of all kinds, in particular those exotic species which reminded her of her childhood on the island of Martinique, and roses, of which she was always especially fond. She began to amass a great collection of plants, some of which she grew from seed sent to her by her family, others from the Jardin des Plantes in Paris and from Kew in London. Redouté was given the run of the place and spent much time painting both outside and in the magnificent hot-houses, and in due course Joséphine started to pay him a generous salary for his work.

In 1800 Redouté's great friend and mentor, L'Héritier, was brutally murdered in the street near his own house. This must have been a severe blow to Redouté, as he and L'Héritier had always remained in close touch and were constantly planning new projects together. Through L'Héritier, Redouté had met nearly all the patrons and friends for whom he worked, and his value in ensuring Redouté's fame cannot be doubted. In other ways, however, Redouté was just embarking on probably the most creative years of his life; his work on *Les Liliacées* (which, together with his later paintings of roses was to become one of his most well-known publications), the vellums, and his work at Malmaison were all to prove successful, and in addition, his talent was recognized internationally.

The first instalment of *Les Liliacées*, painted and

Streptopus amplexifolius (L.) D.C.

This elegant plant, a relative of the Solomon's seal, and of the lily-of-the-valley, is found in Europe, North America and eastern Asia, growing in damp woods, usually in the mountains. The stems may be three feet tall, and are usually much branched, rather than the simple stem shown here.

Streptopus amplexifolius is the only European species, but a second one, *Streptopus roseus* is found in North America. It is smaller, with pink bells, and is even more graceful and dainty.

published by Redouté himself, was published in 1802. This massive work, consisting of 486 plates, each accompanied by an explanatory text, took fourteen years to complete, and is considered by many to be not only his most excellent publication, but also one of the greatest illustrated botanical books ever published. Redouté was assisted in its production by three botanists, firstly, de Candolle (with whom he had worked on the *Histoire Naturelle des Plantes Grasses*), followed by François Delaroche and finally, Alire Raffenau-Delile. Around two hundred copies were published, and each plate was carefully hand-finished with watercolour after printing. As *Les Liliacées* appeared in eighty parts, and was sold on subscription, it was important for the economic success of the book that the advance issue was well-subscribed. Once again, Redouté was fortunate in having an interested and influential patron (Joséphine) who was able to help him both by personal support and by using her contacts to ensure that a sufficient number of people subscribed to ensure the success of the work. Redouté tactfully dedicated the book to the Interior Minister, who subsequently was responsible for ordering eighty sets of each instalment to be used in French museums and as gifts to foreign embassies and so on, to demonstrate the strengths of French culture. In addition to the ordinary sets of the work, eighteen extra large copies were printed and hand-finished by Redouté himself. Naturally these are highly prized by collectors today. Joséphine bought the original paintings for *Les Liliacées*, which were done on vellum, together with a special copy of the text, also on vellum, and these were collected in sixteen volumes. Sadly, this collection has been broken up, after being sold by Sotheby's in New York in 1985.

Uvularia perfoliata L.

In spite of the label given it by Redouté, this plant looks more like *Uvularia grandiflora* J.E. Smith, a larger plant with deeper yellow flowers and longer petals, one to one and a half inches long. The leaves are finely hairy beneath. It grows wild in woods from Quebec westwards to Ontario, and south to Georgia, Tennessee and Kansas, and it is a good plant for a shady place in the garden, but is susceptible to late spring frosts and summer drought. The generic name *Uvularia* refers to the shape of the leaf.

Lilium penduliflorum D.C.

This graceful plant, now known as *Lilium canadense* L., the Canada or meadow lily, was almost certainly the first American lily to be introduced into cultivation in Europe. It was brought over by the French in the early seventeenth century, and was known to John Parkinson, who in his *Paradisus in Sole, Paradisus Terrestris*, a description of, amongst other things, "all sorts of pleasant flowers which our English ayre will permitt to be noursed up" published in 1629, lists "the spotted martagon of Canada".

Lilium canadense is common in Canada and eastern North America from Quebec south to Alabama, where it flourishes in damp meadows, along the edges of streams, and in wet woods, growing amongst ferns. It is not easy to cultivate in Europe, needing rather acid, well-drained soil, which should never be allowed to dry out. Due to its widespread distribution in the wild, there are a number of different forms with flower colours ranging from deep red with conspicuous spots, through orange to an unspotted yellow.

Lilium Penduliflorum *Lis à fleurs pendantes*

P.J. Redouté pinx. de Gouy sculp.

Hemerocallis flava L.

This daylily is now called *Hemerocallis lilioasphodelus* L., and is probably native to China. It was an early introduction to Europe, and is widely naturalized in many places; in the south-eastern foothills of the Alps in Italy and Yugoslavia, it grows wild by rivers and in wet meadows, and may even be native. Other species of *Hemerocallis* are found wild in China and Japan, growing in moist meadows in the mountains or by the sea, often in countless thousands. Many of the named species are difficult to tell apart, varying mainly in height, root thickness and branching.

Most of the cultivated daylilies have been raised from the orange-flowered *Hemerocallis fulva*, by careful selection of different colour breaks and seedlings with wide petals. They are now available in shades of red, pink, mauve and white, as well as the original yellows and oranges.

Hemerocallis Flava.   *Hemerocalle Jaune.*

Amaryllis aurea L.

The genus *Lycoris* Herb., to which this plant belongs, has seven or eight species of this beautiful genus, which is related to *Nerine* and *Amaryllis*. All are native to China and Japan, and may be conspicuous on the banks between paddy fields in late summer and autumn. This species, known as the golden spider lily, was first described by L'Héritier, Redouté's friend and mentor; it is thought to originate in Japan and Formosa, and possibly China also, where it grows in rather open, sunny places. Unfortunately it does not really flourish as a garden plant in Britain, due to the lack of sufficient summer heat, although it can withstand a few degrees of frost and may be grown in sheltered positions in milder parts of the country. A sunny bed in a cool greenhouse may prove more congenial, and more productive of the flowers, which appear in August and September.

Crinum americanum L.

The genus *Crinum* is one of the largest in the *Amaryllidaceae*, containing about 130 species, and found in every tropical continent, usually growing in wet places and often partially submerged in swamps or rivers. It is only absent from Europe, though some of the hardier South African species such as *Crinum moorei* will grow outside as far north as England.

The species shown here is native to North America, and found in the warmer south-eastern states, growing in marshes and wet places. The large flowers are sweetly scented, about eight inches across, and the leaves about three feet long, arising from a large bulb.

Crinum Americanum   *Crinum d'Amérique*

Agapanthus umbellatus L'Héritier

The genus *Agapanthus* consists of ten species and ten subspecies of perennial herbs, which have short creeping rootstocks and thick fleshy roots. These very handsome plants are all native of southern Africa, and many are not reliably hardy in Britain; the most successful method of cultivation for the tender species is to keep them in large pots or tubs, which can be moved indoors during the winter. There is a considerable degree of variation in flower colour, ranging from white through light to dark blue, and most of the plants now in cultivation are hybrids. The plant shown here is now known as *Agapanthus africanus* (L.) Hoffmgg., which is one of the tender evergreen species, found wild on the Cape peninsula and eastwards. The hardier species are from the summer rainfall area of Natal and Transvaal, and are deciduous in winter, and it was from these that the 'Headbourne hybrids' were raised.

Agapanthus Umbellatus   *Agapanthe en Ombelle.*

Commelina tuberosa L.

This attractive garden plant is now known as *Commelina coelestis* Willd., a name which aptly describes the vivid blue flowers, which open in the morning and fade by the evening; fortunately a succession emerge from each bract. It is a native of Mexico, where it tends to grow at high altitudes enjoying cool conditions, and it is thus able to survive outside in warm parts of Britain, although it generally needs to be brought indoors in the winter in cooler areas. Its tuberous roots can be treated in the same way as those of a dahlia. The genus *Commelina* is a large one, containing over two hundred species, most of which are tropical or subtropical, although it is related to the North American *Tradescantia*, which is hardy.

Commelina takes its name from Caspar (1667–1731) and his uncle Jan Commelin (1629–1698), Dutch botanists; Jan, author of *The Belgick or Netherlandish Hesperides*, a fine book published in 1676, and translated into English in 1683, was a civilized and wealthy merchant from Amsterdam, who was in charge of the city's Physic Garden. Jan Commelin started, and his nephew Caspar completed, the two-volume florilegium entitled *Horti Medici Amstelodamensis Rariorum Plantarum Descriptio et Icones*, (A description and illustrations of rare plants of the Physic Garden in Amsterdam), which contains 230 engravings of rare and exotic plants, and was published from 1697–1701.

Les Roses. The first edition of *Les Roses, décrites et classées selon leur ordre naturel par Claude Antoine Thory*, was published in three folio volumes from 1817–1824. This was Redouté's second foray into publishing, his first such venture being the publication of the very successful *Les Liliacées*. It is a magnificent work, containing 167 engravings, of a somewhat stylized elegance. The text was contributed by Claude Antoine Thory (1759–1827), a lawyer and friend of Redouté, who was a keen amateur botanist. A second edition of the book, also in three parts, but with only 160 plates, was published between 1824 and 1826 by M. Panckoucke (also a friend of Redouté, and a rather better businessman!), and this was followed by a third edition in 1828–1830.

Iris pallida Lam.

This iris is one of the most important parents of the modern bearded irises which are so popular in gardens both in Europe and in North America. It is native along the coast of the Adriatic in northern Italy and Yugoslavia, and we have seen it growing in great quantity on limestone cliffs and rock ledges on the road which leads down to the coast near Titograd.

Iris pallida may be distinguished from other species by its completely papery, whitish bracts. The leaves are broad and glaucous green, and are a fine feature even when the flowering season has passed. The flowers are freely produced, and are usually of a pure lilac-blue colour. Redouté's *Les Liliacées* is of great interest to anyone wanting to study the early history of bearded irises, for it illustrates with great accuracy not only the species on which the modern hybrids have been based, but the early garden hybrids whose origins are unrecorded.

Iris pallida.   *Iris pâle.*

Limodorum grandiflorum AUBL.

This large terrestrial orchid is now called *Phaius tankervilleae* (Banks) Blume. It was one of the first tropical orchids to be cultivated in Europe, as it is recorded that it was introduced by an agent of Dr John Fothergill from China in 1778. As it was first described by Sir Joseph Banks in L'Héritier's *Sertum Anglicum* as *Limodorum tankervillae*, Redouté probably first saw this orchid during his visit to London. The specific name celebrates Charles Bennet, fourth Earl of Tankerville, who had a garden at Walton-on-Thames, Surrey, and with Dr William Pitcairn, Banks and Fothergill, employed a collector in South Africa, and probably also arranged for cultivated plants to be sent back from China.

The cultivation of tropical orchids, and especially of epiphytes, proved difficult for the early gardeners, and by the time Redouté had finished the plates of *Les Liliacées* in 1816, he had illustrated only nine tropical orchids, *Encyclia cochleata* from Florida south to Venezuela, *Epidendrum ciliare* from the West Indies, and two cymbidiums and *Bletia verecunda*, already commonly cultivated in China.

The flowering stems of *Phaius tankervillae* may reach six feet, and the fan of leaves is three feet or more tall; each flower may be five inches across, and there may be twenty on a spike. It is now known to be widely distributed in the lowland forests of eastern Asia, from north India to Ceylon, China, Indonesia and northern Australia.

CHAPTER IV

REDOUTÉ AT MALMAISON

Throughout the time that Redouté was working on *Les Liliacées*, he was also busy at Malmaison, recording the huge variety of plants that grew there. In 1803 the first instalment of *Jardin de la Malmaison*, in which 120 rare plants grown at Malmaison were illustrated by Redouté and described by E.P. Ventenat, was published. Redouté was also meanwhile giving painting lessons to fashionable young ladies in Paris, who paid highly for the privilege of learning from the master.

In May 1804, Napoleon crowned himself first Emperor of France, and Joséphine became Empress. At about this time, Joséphine began to pay Redouté a substantial salary, which gave him the means to purchase an estate for himself, at Fleury-Meudon south of Paris, where he was at last able to indulge his love of plants. Redouté soon learnt that the famous and eccentric political philosopher, essayist, composer and botanist, Jean Jacques Rousseau (1712–1778) had been well-known in the neighbourhood, where he had taken refuge with the liberal-minded Marquis de Mirabeau. Years before, L'Héritier had suggested to Redouté that he might one day illustrate Rousseau's extraordinary book *La Botanique de J.J. Rousseau*. This new edition of the book, published in 1805, with sixty-four colour plates by Redouté, was a success, although of course it was of no help to the unfortunate Rousseau, who had died insane and poverty-stricken twenty-seven years before. Other books published around this time include the monographs on *Astragalogia* (1802) and *Strophantus* (1804) both in collaboration with de Candolle and published

JARDIN DE LA MALMAISON. The two volumes of *Jardin de la Malmaison*, with 120 plates by Redouté, and text by Étienne Pierre Ventenat, were published in 1803 and 1805. The paintings of rare plants that grew at Malmaison were colour printed and hand finished, making this a very splendid work.

Clethra arborea AIT.

This beautiful large shrub is a native of Madeira, from whence it was introduced to Britain in 1784. Due to a slight resemblance of the pure white scented flowers, this *Clethra* has been given the common name of the lily-of-the-valley tree. It is not easy to grow successfully in Britain, as it requires winter protection in all but the very mildest areas, but the beauty of the flowers, which are borne in panicles during August to October, is such that it is worth taking trouble with it in areas such as Devon, Cornwall, the west coast of Scotland and Ireland. A well-drained, lime-free soil, and protection from cold winds are essential; it is often grown in cooler districts as a greenhouse plant. This is an interesting relic of the Tertiary evergreen forest flora of Europe, now much depleted by the ice ages, but remnants of which survive in the Canaries and Madeira. No other species of *Clethra* are found in Europe, but *Clethra alnifolia* is frequent in eastern North America, and several other species are found in China.

1   2   3   4   5   6   7   8   9

by Garnery; the *Histoire des chênes de l'Amérique* (1801), by André Michaux, illustrated by both Redouté and his younger brother, Henri-Joseph; and the *Traité des Arbres et Arbustes, que l'on cultive en plein terre en France* (known as the *Nouveau Duhamel*, as it was an expanded and revised edition of an earlier work), in collaboration with Duhamel de Monceau (1800–1819), although most of Redouté's illustrations were done in 1804.

After a time, Napoleon became obsessed with the idea that he should have an heir, and as Joséphine was unable to provide him with one, the marriage was dissolved in December 1809, although Joséphine retained the title of Empress and was given the estate at Malmaison and a large allowance. Thereafter, perhaps to alleviate the loneliness she felt at losing Napoleon, Joséphine's enthusiasm for her garden, and for roses in particular, seems to have increased to the point where it became her main interest in life.

Napoleon also presented Joséphine with a further château, Navarre, near Evreux, in Normandy; the reason for this is not clear, but as Napoleon was busily looking around for a new wife, he may have felt that the presence of Joséphine and her attendant crowd of friends and admirers at Malmaison was a bit too close to Paris for comfort.

Although this property was as neglected as Malmaison had once been, Joséphine appears to have contrived to make another wonderful garden, with hot-houses full of rare plants. Navarre, however, never seems to have occupied the same position in her affections as Malmaison. Redouté travelled occasionally to Normandy to paint the flowers there, and in 1813, a further publication, *Description des plantes rares cultivées à Malmaison et à Navarre*, with fifty-four particularly splendid plates by Redouté, and a text by Aimé Bonpland, was published; this was engraved with the colour stipple technique perfected by Re-

---

Dionaea muscipula Ellis

Venus's fly-trap, as this plant is commonly known, is one of the insectivorous plants which trap flies by closing their leaves when the leaf lobe is firmly touched or one of the central bristles is lightly depressed a couple of times. The flies are digested, and the plant absorbs the resulting nitrogen. There are many other carnivorous plants, some of which (e.g. the sundew, *Drosera*) have mobile sticky hairs; others catch insects by means of underwater traps (e.g. bladderwort *Utricularia*), while yet others, such as the pitcher plants, have traps which do not move – the insects crawl into the pitcher-shaped bladder of the plant and are unable to escape.

Dionaea is an herbaceous perennial, native of North Carolina, where it grows in damp mossy places on moist sandy soil; it spreads by underground stems. The white flowers are borne in an umbel during July and August, and in shady areas the leaves are green, whereas in sunny places the leaves are red with a green margin. It can be grown in a pot in a compost of fine silver sand and peat, surrounded by live sphagnum moss; the pot should stand in water so that the roots remain moist, and be kept as cold as possible in winter.

1   *2*   *3*   *4*

douté, and hand-finished.

In April 1810, Napoleon married the young Archduchess Marie Louise of Austria (incidentally a great niece of Marie-Antoinette), and in the following year a son was born, later to become King of Rome and the Duke of Reichstadt. Relations between the two Empresses were not cordial, due more, it would appear, to the immaturity of Marie-Louise than to any jealous feelings that might not unreasonably have been felt by Joséphine. This did not, however, stop the new Empress from commanding Redouté to give her lessons in flower painting at the Palace of the Tuileries.

In 1812 the French army was forced to make its disastrous retreat from Moscow, and this, together with a long series of military disasters, forced Napoleon to abdicate, first in favour of his son, and then unconditionally. He was given the sovereignty of Elba and allowed to retain the title of Emperor, but he could not resist another attempt to regain his old powers, and invaded France in 1815. Only after his final defeat at the Battle of Waterloo was he banished to the island of St Helena, where he died in 1821.

Joséphine herself died suddenly in the summer of 1814. After Napoleon's abdication her income was reduced somewhat, but she continued to live in style, and kept her gardens up as before. After her death, it was discovered that she had amassed the most enormous debts, so her children by her first marriage had to sell much of her property, but they kept Malmaison for a time, and Redouté continued to visit the garden and paint, although of course he was no longer salaried. It was Joséphine's enormous collection of roses which inspired Redouté to attempt to paint every variety of rose that then grew in France, a project that was finally completed in 1824.

Echium grandiflorum ANDREWS

Now called *Lobostemon grandiflorus* (Andrews) Levyns, this small shrub is native to the Cape area of South Africa, around Stellenbosch. It was introduced into cultivation in England in 1787, but is now rarely, if ever cultivated. There are twenty-eight species of *Lobostemon* in South Africa, most of which are shrubs, with red, pink or blue flowers, and several were grown in greenhouses in the nineteenth century.

True *Echium* species, called viper's bugloss, are native to Europe, West Asia and North Africa, and are mostly annuals or perennials. Several shrubby species are found in the Canary Islands and Madeira, and they make fine plants for cool greenhouses, or gardens in Mediterranean climates.

Josephinia imperatricis VENTENAT

It is surprising that Ventenat chose this obscure plant, a native of the Celebes south to northern Australia, to honour his patron, the Empress Joséphine. It is a relative of the foxglove-like plant, *Sesamum indicum*, from which sesame seeds are obtained.

Napoleona imperialis from the rainforest of southern Nigeria, is almost as obscure, but is sometimes cultivated, making a shrub or small tree with unusual blue and pink flowers, with four series of stamens in concentric circles. Joséphine had already had one of the most beautiful of all flowering plants named after her, *Lapageria rosea*, the national flower of Chile, a climber with large, waxy bells of rich crimson. It was named by Ruiz and Pavon in 1802, taking her maiden name, Tascher de la Pagerie.

Nymphaea caerulea SAVIGNY

This spectacular waterlily is common in the Nile delta, and is found as far south as Central Africa. It was not scientifically named until 1803, by M. de Savigny, a member of the Institute of Egypt, and its cultivation in northern Europe seems to date from this time, although it was greatly appreciated by the ancient Egyptians for thousands of years prior to this; it is the famous Lotus of the Nile.

Redouté's younger brother Henri-Joseph was a member of the Institute of Egypt which accompanied the French army under Napoleon, when it entered Egypt in 1798. This team of scientists, scholars, engineers and artists was commissioned to make a detailed survey of all aspects of Egypt, including its flora, fauna and geographical features, and to record and illustrate everything they found in the form of a huge encyclopaedia. After the Battle of the Nile, in which the French fleet was decimated by Nelson, the French were effectively kept under siege by the English, but the members of the Institute continued with their work for over three years, until the signing of a peace treaty with England in 1802. Their great work, *Description de l'Egypte*, was published in twenty volumes from 1809–1825. Henri-Joseph contributed over fifty sketches and paintings of a great variety of Egyptian artefacts, animals and plants, including the fish of the Nile; in Egypt also, Henri-Joseph contracted the severe eye disease that eventually curtailed his career as an artist.

Platylobium formosum Smith

This attractive Australian shrub is native to New South Wales and Tasmania, where it grows in similar situations to the hardier of the wattles such as *Acacia baileyana* and *Acacia dealbata*. It forms a shrub four to five feet high, and flowers in mid-summer. Although it was grown at Malmaison in 1800, and in England at the same time, it is now very rare or absent from European and American gardens. It would make a good garden shrub in California, and Redouté himself found it so attractive that he included a reduced version of this plate in the *Choix des plus belles fleurs*.

1   2   3   4   5

Euphorbia mellifera Ait.

This handsome spurge is native of the Canaries, where it grows in evergreen forests in the mountains. Although very rare in the wild, it is easily grown in gardens and is nearly hardy, surviving about minus 10°C of frost.

In due course it will make a large shrub or small tree, with rather fleshy and woody stems. Other shrubby spurges are found along the Mediterranean coast, but they are even less tolerant of cold. *Euphorbia mellifera* forms a link between the herbaceous species which are commonest in Europe, and the tree-like succulent African species, some of which are also found in the Canaries, growing in particularly desert areas near the coast. Its specific name suggests that it is a good source of honey. Mount Hymettus near Athens, famous in antiquity for its honey, is covered with the spiny cushions of *Euphorbia acanthothamnos*, bright yellow in spring with honey-scented flowers. The flowers of spurges have an unusual structure, with three main components; a single female flower with a three-chambered ovary on a short curved stalk, with three styles; numerous male flowers each with a single forked stamen; and a ring of nectar-bearing glands which may be circular, oval, horned or even comb-like. The whole is surrounded by pairs or whorls of coloured bracts, usually yellow or greenish, but often red and conspicuous, and sometimes even white or brownish.

Euphorbia Mellifera

TRAITÉ DES ARBRES ET ARBUSTES. The second, revised edition of *Traité des Arbres et Arbustes, que l'on cultive en pleine terre en France* (Treatise on the Trees and Shrubs which may be grown in the open ground in France) and often known merely as the *Nouveau Duhamel*, by Henri Louis Duhamel du Monceau, was published in Paris from 1800–1819. The seven volumes (the first of which was dedicated to 'Madame Bonaparte' – she did not become Empress until 1804) contain 498 plates, printed in colour using the stipple technique, and retouched by hand. Redouté supplied most of the paintings for the first five volumes, and one of his pupils, Pancrace Bessa (1772–1835) illustrated the remaining two volumes.

Apricotier commun

The common apricot, *Prunus armeniaca* L., is a native of central Asia and northern and western China, and has long been cultivated for its delicious fruit. It was known to Pliny in the first century A.D., and was probably cultivated by the Romans during their occupation of Britain. History is vague as regards the intervening period, but in 1524 a gardener to Henry VIII is reported to have brought a number of trees from Italy. By the sixteenth century walled gardens containing many kinds of fruits and vegetables were being described by writers such as Celia Fiennes, who mentions 'apricocke, peach, plum and necktarine', as well as cherries and strawberries. Shakespeare, in Richard II, gave the apricot an honourable mention:

> 'Go, bind thou up yon dangling apricocks,
> Which, like unruly children, make their sire
> Stoop with oppression of their prodigal weight'.

2

ARMENIACA vulgaris.　　ABRICOTIER commun.

J. Redouté pinx.　　　　　　　　　　　　　　　　Lemaire sculp.

Cerisier

There are three types of cherry cultivated for fruit: the Sweet, *Prunus avium* L., which is native to Britain, the Sour, *Prunus cerasus* L., thought to originate in western Asia, and the Duke, *Prunus x gonduini*. Sour cherries are sub-divided into two groups, the Morellos, which have red-fleshed fruit, and the Amarelles with yellowish flesh; the Dukes are hybrids between the Morello and the Sweet cherry. From the foregoing it can be seen that the exact parentage of the edible cherries is obscure, but they have been much appreciated from earliest times. They were certainly known to Theophrastus in the third century B.C., and the Roman General and gourmet Lucullus is supposed to have found a cherry tree at Cerasus in Turkey, and to have brought it back with him to Italy. Whether or not this is true, Pliny states that several varieties were grown in Rome, and the popularity of the cherry spread far and wide throughout the Roman Empire. By the fourteenth century Charles V of France was reported to have planted over a thousand cherry trees in his royal gardens, and there are numerous later references to the popularity of cherries in English literature, from 'Cherry ripe, ripe, ripe, I cry, Full and fair ones, come and buy' (a version of the street-seller's call by Robert Herrick, 1591–1674) to 'Kent, sir – everybody knows Kent – apples, cherries, hops, and women' (Dickens).

CERASUS.   CERISIER.

A. *Guigne piquante*. B. *Griotte de Portugal*. C. *Petite Guigne noire*. D. *Guigne blanche tardive*.

P. J. Redouté pinx.   Lemai

Cobaea scandens Cav.

There are about twenty-two species of *Cobaea*, named after the Spanish Jesuit missionary and naturalist, Father B. Cobo, all of which are native of Central America. *Cobaea scandens*, from southern Mexico, but also naturalized in other South American countries, is the only species to be widely cultivated, and despite being a perennial, in Britain is usually grown as an annual. It thrives in warm sunny sheltered places, and will do well in a greenhouse or conservatory; it is a fast and vigorous grower, and needs some kind of support to cling onto. The bell-shaped flowers are greenish-white at first, becoming mauve and later purple, and there are also cultivars with variegated foliage, and white and deep indigo flowers. The flowers have a strong musky scent when first open, and this attracts pollinating insects; there is some evidence that they may also be pollinated by bats, as bat claw marks have been recorded on a related species, and the broad tubular corolla is characteristic of bat-pollinated flowers.

COBŒA Scandens.

COBŒA Sarmenteux.

P. J. Redouté pinx.

Lemaire Sculp.

Illicium floridanum Ellis

The genus *Illicium* is one of the groups of plants which demonstrate the connections of the floras of Southeast China and Japan, and of eastern North America. Of the roughly forty species of aromatic evergreen trees and shrubs, only three are commonly grown outside in Britain; two, *I. anisatum* and *I. henryi*, from China and Japan, and the other, *I. floridanum*, from America.

Illicium anisatum (often called *I. religiosum*) is often planted by Buddhist temples and in palace courtyards in Japan; it has pale yellow flowers in spring, followed by fruits grouped in a star-like ring. *I. henryi*, from western China, is a medium-sized shrub or small tree, with bright pink flowers. *I. floridanum* is the most attractive of the three when in flower, bearing maroon-purple blooms, with strap-shaped petals, at the end of the shoots in May and June. A native of western Florida, Alabama, Mississippi and Louisiana, it grows by streams and in other moist areas, and is sometimes found in very swampy places. It was apparently first found by John Bartram (1699–1777), a Quaker botanist from Pennsylvania, in 1766, and was introduced to England in 1771. *Illicium floridanum* prefers a warm sheltered position and an acid soil, so does best in the milder counties of Britain.

Koelreuteria paniculata Laxm.

This deciduous tree is a native of northern China, where it was often planted by the graves of the Chinese aristocracy, and by houses, and it is said to be the crooked tree shown on Willow Pattern china. Seven species are known, all from eastern Asia, but only *Koelreuteria paniculata* is commonly cultivated. Although it prefers a sunnier climate, it is quite hardy in Britain, and in high summer the deep yellow flowers can be a striking sight; these are followed by the strange large bladder-like fruits, which turn from pale green to pink and then brown. The leaves are also conspicuous in the autumn, often turning a bright yellow; at one time they were used by the Chinese to produce a kind of black dye. *Koelreuteria*, named after J.G. Koelreuter (1733–1806) Professor of Natural History at Karlsruhe, and a friend and correspondent of Linnaeus, was first introduced into England in 1763, and a number of fine old specimens can be seen today, notably at Syon House, and the Chelsea Physic Garden, London.

KOELREUTERIA paniculata.

KOELREUTERIA paniculé. *pag.165*

P.J.Redouté pinx.

J.Marchand Sc.

Sorbus domestica L.

The service tree, as this is commonly known, is a large tree reaching up to fifty feet (rarely, seventy) in height, and resembles a huge mountain ash, to which it is related. It is a native of southern and eastern Europe, eastwards to the Caucasus mountains and North Africa. It has leaves up to nine inches long, and bears small white flowers during late spring. The green fruits, which are apple or pear-shaped, depending on the form of the tree, can be eaten as they rot, rather like a medlar, although we have not tried them ourselves, and they do not sound very appetizing. According to William Cobbett, writing in *The English Gardener* in 1833, 'It is totally unfit to be eaten', but despite this, it had been grown in Italy as a dessert fruit for years, being much esteemed especially by the Romans. No-one seems to know exactly when the tree was introduced into Britain, although one might well assume that the Romans were responsible, and the fruits were certainly eaten here until well into the eighteenth century, when Furber illustrated both the 'Italian Service' and the 'English Service' in his calendar catalogue. The best examples of large service trees to be seen today are in the Oxford Botanic Garden, where they are thought to have been planted by John Sibthorp, Professor of Botany at Oxford from 1784–1795.

T. 3. N.º 34.

SORBUS domestica.

J. Redouté pinx.

SORBIER domestique. *pag. 142.*

Gabriel Sculp.

Sparmannia africana L. FIL.

The genus *Sparmannia* is named after Dr Anders Sparrman (1748–1820), a Swedish traveller who accompanied Captain Cook on his second voyage and botanized in the Cape from 1772–1776. There are about seven species, natives of tropical and South Africa; *Sparmannia africana*, introduced to Britain in 1790, is an attractive small tree or shrub which grows on the edge of forests, near rivers and in other moist places in the eastern Cape, and can only be grown under glass in Britain. It is quick-growing, and bears delicate, short-lived white flowers with sensitive stamens, which respond to touch. In South Africa it is known as African hemp, because of its fibrous bark, but in Germany it is called Zimmer Linden, meaning room-lime, from the fact that it has long been a popular houseplant and is a member of the lime family.

SPARMANNIA Africana.   **SPARMANNIA d'Afrique.**

P. J. Redouté pinx.

Lemaire sculp.

La Botanique. A volume of botanical writings by the eccentric philosopher, writer and botanist Jean Jacques Rousseau (1712–1778), was published by Delachaussee & Garnery in 1805. The circumstances in which Redouté produced drawings for this book are described in the introduction.

An Oak Tree and a Rose Bush

This is one of the few published plates by Redouté which shows whole plants as they grow. It demonstrates the growth forms of woody plants, a tree, in this case an oak, and a large shrub, here a wild rose, and a small shrub, a *Cistus*. Apart from his general philosophical works, such as holding that art and science polluted mankind by seducing him from his natural and noble estate, his music and operas, and his educational theories, Rousseau was a keen amateur botanist in later life, and great admirer of Linnaeus, whom he considered 'the best interpreter of the works of nature'.

Description des plantes rares cultiviées à Malmaison et à Navarre. Descriptions of rare plants cultivated at Malmaison and at Navarre by Aimé Jacques Bonpland (1773–1858), was published in Paris from 1812–1817. Of the sixty-four colour stipple engravings, nine were drawn by Bessa, with the remainder by Redouté, and each plate was hand-finished. Bonpland was both a surgeon and a botanist, who had accompanied Alexander von Humboldt (after whom the current is named) on his expedition to Central and South America a few years previously.

Cactus ambiguus Bonpl.

Now known as *Nyctocereus serpentinus* Britton & Rose, the snake cactus, is a native of Mexico, as also is the very similar, and closely related, *Peniocereus greggii*, a native of Mexico, New Mexico and Arizona. The name is derived from *nyktos* = night, as the genus consists of night-flowering species; the large, white flowers are thought to be pollinated by moths.

Cactus Ambiguus.

Chorizema ilicifolia LA BILL.

The genus *Chorizema* consists of about twenty species of evergreen shrubs and sub-shrubs, all of which are native to western Australia. J.J.H. de La Billardière, a botanist who had joined D'Entecastaux's expedition to western Australia, when they were searching for La Perouse, a French sailor-explorer who vanished in the Antipodes, was said to have chosen the name, derived from choros, a dance, and zema, a drink, because he was so thrilled to discover a spring of fresh water near where the plant grew; most of the springs in the area being brackish. The epithet *ilicifolia* refers to the holly-like leaves. This is one of the smallest species, sometimes prostrate in habit, and like the other members of the genus, has flowers of an unusual combination of colours – orange, red, crimson and yellow. La Billardière (1755–1834) wrote three important botanical books: *Icones plantarum Syriae rariorum* (1791–1812), containing very fine black and white engravings by both the Redouté brothers, Turpin and Poiteau; *Novae Hollandiae plantarum specimen* (1804–1806), with 265 pictures of Australian plants by Poiteau, Turpin and others, and a flora of New Caledonia (1824–1825) with eighty engravings by Turpin.

Chorizema Ilicifolia.

Digitalis × purpurascens ROTH.

This interesting foxglove is a hybrid between the common pinkish-purple foxglove, *Digitalis × purpurea*, a native of western and central Europe, and the mainly eastern European *D. lutea*, which has numerous small yellow flowers. The hybrid is sterile, and found wild in places where the parents grow together, for instance in Spain, southern France and Germany. It is perennial, and an attractive garden plant with numerous rather small flowers of an unusual shade of creamy-pink.

A second hybrid foxglove is commoner as a garden plant. This is *Digitalis × mertonensis*, a cross between *D. purpurea* and the large yellow-flowered, *D. grandiflora*. This fertile hybrid species was created at the John Innes Institute, at that time in Merton, Surrey, and was originally sterile. Sterile hybrids between species can be made fertile by treatment with colchicine, a very poisonous alkaloid extracted from *Colchicum* leaves. By interfering with the formation of cell walls during cell division, colchicine produces cells with double the number of chromosomes, and these cells can grow into a complete plant, which is fertile, able to set seed and behave as a new species. A recent cross, between *D. lutea* and *D. × mertonensis*, has been named 'Glory of Roundway' after the Wiltshire garden in which it appeared.

Digitalis Purpurascens

Erica grandiflora L. FIL.

This is one of the finest of the six hundred or so species of heathers from the Cape region of South Africa. It is found on dry stony mountains from near Cape Town to the edges of the Great Karoo desert, forming a shrub to 1.5 m tall, and with flowers up to 2.8 cm long. To the Europeans of the eighteenth century, who knew only about ten of the twenty species of northern hemisphere heathers, mostly with small pinkish flowers, the diversity and beauty of the Cape species were a wonderful surprise, and they soon became popular in greenhouses and much cultivated and hybridized.

Erica Grandiflora.

P. J. Redouté 1811.

2. 3. 4. 5.

Lobelia excelsa BONPL.

This handsome lobelia is now called *Lobelia tupa* L., and is native of the southern part of South America, growing in sandy places near the coast, especially in Argentina and Chile, where it can make large clumps of stems to twelve feet high. This height is not usually reached in cultivation, where six feet is normal; it needs a sunny position and well-drained soil, and can survive about minus 10°C if the rootstock is protected. The plant is very poisonous, and even the dust from the dead stems is harmful if inhaled. The stiff red flowers are adapted for pollination by humming-birds.

The name 'tupa' is derived from the Indian name for the plant, and Linnaeus probably saw the specimens collected in Chile by Father Louis Feuillée in around 1710. Feuillée spent four years in Chile and Peru, and published an account of the medicinal plants of the area in 1714.

The plant was not introduced into cultivation until later, being recorded in cultivation in England in 1824, though Redouté's painting dates from before 1817. It is probable that it was introduced by Bonpland himself, who travelled in South America with Alexander von Humboldt from June 1799 to early 1804.

Lobelia Excelsa.

Magnolia macrophylla MICHX.

The genus *Magnolia* consists of about eighty evergreen trees and shrubs, named after Pierre Magnol (1638–1751), professor of botany and medicine and Director of the Botanic Gardens at Montpellier. About half the species are tropical, and are native of East and Southeast Asia, and the Himalaya, although many of the temperate species, most of which have been introduced to Britain, come from northern and Central America.

Magnolia macrophylla is a deciduous tree which was discovered in South Carolina and described by André Michaux in 1759; it was introduced to Europe in 1800. It has remarkably large leaves, sometimes three feet long, the upper sides of which are bright green, while the underside is silvery-grey and downy. The beautiful large fragrant flowers are creamy-white, with purple markings in the centre, and appear in early summer. This lovely magnolia is best given a rather sheltered position as it can be susceptible to frost, and the huge soft leaves can be damaged by wind.

Magnolia Macrophylla.

CHAPTER V

LES ROSES AND
LATER PUBLICATIONS

May 1814 saw the return of the monarchy to France after an interval of 25 years. King Louis XVIII, and his niece, Marie-Antoinette's daughter, arrived in Paris, then occupied by troops from Russia, Prussia, Austria and England. Other aristocrats who had fled abroad, now began to drift back to France, and a number of them enrolled their daughters as pupils with Redouté. He was still contributing paintings to the *vélins*, and continued to bring out instalments of *Les Liliacées*, while beginning to work on his new project, *Les Roses*. For this he had engaged the help of a friend and botanist, Claude Antoine Thory, a keen gardener and lover of roses. The two men travelled all over France, looking for different species and varieties of roses to include in their book, and in the early days, Redouté painted roses from Malmaison also.

Louis XVIII had turned out to be something of a disappointment, and on hearing that Napoleon had escaped from Elba and was marching to Paris he fled to Belgium. After Napoleon's defeat at Waterloo, and his subsequent banishment to St Helena, Louis returned to Paris, and decided that he could no longer tolerate any of Napoleon's family or sympathizers – they were not to be trusted. Because of this, Hortense, Joséphine's daughter by her first marriage, was forced to flee the country, and the estate of Malmaison, including all the contents of the house and much of the garden, was sold. Almost the only records of the enormous variety of plants once grown there by Joséphine were Redouté's paintings, and the two books published in 1803 and 1813.

The first instalment of *Les Roses* was published in 1817, and although it is today probably the best

---

Metrosyderos glauca BONPL.

This bottle brush, now known as *Callistemon speciosus* DC., is a native of western Australia, New Zealand and Polynesia, and was introduced to England in 1823. The name *Callistemon* is derived from kallos = beauty, and stemon = stamen, and the beauty of the flowers is indeed almost entirely due to the very numerous long stamens. It makes a large shrub or small tree up to fifteen feet high, and is suitable for growing outside only in the very mildest areas of Britain and North America, although it makes a fine plant for the cool greenhouse or conservatory; it will also do well if kept in pots or tubs and plunged outside during the summer. *Callistemon speciosus* produces its wonderful bright red flowers, with golden anthers, from May to July, but young specimens take some time to become established and to flower freely.

P. J. Redouté 1812.

Metrosyderos Glauca.

known of all Redouté's work, at the time he experienced some difficulty in attracting enough subscribers for it. This was due in part to the fact that Joséphine and Napoleon had supported his earlier publications both by subscribing themselves, and by encouraging others to do so too. Without their patronage, Redouté had to work harder to find interested buyers for what was a very costly work. Nevertheless, Redouté continued the publication, producing 169 plates in thirty volumes over the years, until the last instalment appeared in 1824. However this venture was proving to be something of a millstone, and he began to be seriously financially embarrassed, although he always just managed to stave off bankruptcy.

During the years in which Redouté was working on *Les Roses*, he also collaborated with André and François André Michaux, father and son. André (1746–1802) had been on an important expedition to the Levant, and sent back seeds of many new plants to Sir Joseph Banks (q.v.), Le Monnier and the Jardin des Plantes in Paris. The Michaux family settled in America, and from there they made many expeditions, collecting seeds, before returning to France in 1796. On the voyage home, they were shipwrecked, losing most of their belongings. In dire financial straits, Michaux struggled to produce his *Histoire des chênes de L'Amérique*, which was eventually published in 1801, but his most important work, the *Flora boreali-americana*, in two volumes, was published after his death by his son. François-André also produced, between 1810 and 1813, the *Histoires des arbres forestiers de L'Amérique septentrionale*, in twenty-four parts, with 140 plates by Redouté and one of his pupils, Pancrace Bessa; an English translation of this, *The North American Sylva*, was published in Philadelphia in 1818–1819.

In 1822 Redouté's younger daughter, Adelaide, a promising young painter of flowers herself, died, probably of a brain tumour. Not surprisingly, this cast a gloom over the Redouté household, and it seemed

Metrosyderos glauca BONPL.

This plate shows the printed version of the original painting shown on the previous page. The plant is now called *Callistemon speciosus* DC. The traditional format of the *vélins* has been abandoned in the printing, and the frame omitted. In many later paintings, such as those for the *Les Liliacées*, after about eighteen, Redouté ceased to put the frame on the original paintings. The original of this plate was painted in 1812, the printed version published in 1813.

A comparison of these two plates shows the accuracy of the engravers who worked in Redouté's studio, but even so, some of the exceptional delicacy of the painting of the stamens of the flower has been lost.

In many botanical plates, the engraver copies the original painting onto the copper plate, so that the print is a mirror image of the original; this did not satisfy Redouté, who insisted that the engravers use a complicated system of mirrors, so that the print appears the same way round as the original painting.

Metrosideros Glauca.

that, after all the good years, things were not going their way. Also in 1822, Gérard van Spaëndonck, probably the greatest artistic influence in Redouté's life, died, and it was announced that in the interests of economy the Chair which he had held at the Jardin des Plantes was to be discontinued. Two posts were to be created in its place, one with responsibility for all matters pertaining to botanical illustration, and the other to deal with all zoological matters. Redouté was awarded the first job, and he became responsible not only for maintaining and adding to the collection of *vélins*, but also for giving lessons in the Jardin des Plantes, all in return for rather a small salary. These public lessons proved so popular with the well-to-do Parisiennes, as well as with those who were really interested in learning the techniques of flower painting, that he was soon asked to give more private lessons. Amongst his pupils were two daughters of the Duc d'Orléans, and Redouté was soon on

good terms with the entire Orléans family. In 1824 Louis XVIII died, leaving the throne to his reactionary brother Charles X, who reigned until his abdication in 1830. Redouté had become friendly with Charles's daughter-in-law, the Duchesse de Berry, and in 1824 he dedicated his *Album de Redouté* (a selection of paintings from *Les Liliacées* and *Les Roses*) to her. This friendship was to stand him in good stead, as in 1828 the Duchess persuaded Charles (after much haggling over the price) to purchase the original watercolours for *Les Roses* for her. The sum paid for these (30,000 francs) must have been a welcome windfall for Redouté, although he was still in dire straits financially, and seemed unable, perhaps after years of Joséphine's extravagant influence, to economize.

In 1824, Redouté made another selection of forty plates from *Les Liliacées*, and brought out his *Choix des quarante plus belles fleurs*. This was followed, in

Mimulus luteus L.

There are about seventy species of the monkey flower, so-called because of the supposed similarity of the corolla to a monkey (mimo = ape). Two species, very similar and frequently hybridizing where they grow together, have been confused under the name M. *luteus*; M. *luteus* L., which is native to the southern hemisphere and was first collected in Chile in 1707, and M. *guttatus* D.C., depicted here, which is native to the western coast of North America, from Mexico and California north to Alaska.

Both M. *guttatus*, which has softly hairy flower stalks and small red spots on the corolla, and M. *luteus*, with hairless flower stalks and large red or purplish blotches on the flower can be found in Britain, although M. *guttatus* is much more common, especially in Scotland. This plant flourishes in wet meadows, by springs, and along the banks of streams and rivers, and has become naturalized both here and in eastern North America. It was introduced into Europe during the early nineteenth century by George H. von Langsdorff (1774–1852), a surgeon and naturalist who was a member of Krustentern's expedition round the world in 1803–1806, although seed had in fact already been sent back by Archibald Menzies (1754–1842), a Scottish surgeon and naturalist, in 1790–1795. It is popular as a plant for bog gardens, but is exceptionally invasive, and in the *Flora of Gloucestershire* (1948) naturalized forms are described as "spreading rapidly in places, threatening to overwhelm the native vegetation".

Mimulus Luteus

1827, by the first instalment of his *Choix des plus belles fleurs*, a selection of 144 plates of flowers, chosen more for their aesthetic value than for their scientific interest. In his Preface he said prophetically: "Illustration of the plant kingdom, or the art of painting plants, to which I have devoted my studies and my life's labours, which has brought me success commensurate with my works, and whose principles I like to demonstrate in the practical course which I give each year at the Muséum du Jardin du Roi, is no less useful than it is pleasurable. . . . Plant illustration, so desirable moreover for the study of botany, gracefully embellishes the finest products of industry . . .". This book was intended to provide models for students of flower painting, and Redouté would probably have been amazed if he could have foreseen the countless replicas of his work in most countries of the world. However, in addition to this professed purpose of the book, one can also assume that in his last major work poor Redouté was desperately trying to raise more cash, a continual preoccupation of his later years. After his forays into publishing, Redouté had decided to place all his future work in the hands of a publisher, Monsieur Panckoucke, a neighbour of his at Fleury-Meudon, who published the later editions of *Les Roses* and the *Choix*.

On the abdication of Charles X, in 1830, the former Duc d'Orléans ascended the throne as King Louis-Philippe I, known, because of his liberal views, as the Citizen-King. Shortly after this, Redouté was

---

Paeonia moutan Sims

This tree paeony, now called *Paeonia suffruticosa* Andr., was introduced into England from China in the eighteenth century, where it had been cultivated and developed in gardens since the seventh century A.D.; the Chinese also valued it as a medicinal plant. Both the Chinese and the Japanese raised many different varieties, but it was not until 1787 that Sir Joseph Banks planted the first variety, a double form known as 'Banksii', to be introduced to England. This plant, which was sent to Banks by an employee of the East India Company, flowered at Kew, and is reported to have reached eight feet high; it survived until 1842.

The true wild form, described as having 'dark and rich magenta crimson' flowers, was found in Shensi, China, by the plant collector William Purdom in 1910, and, while travelling with Reginald Farrer, he came upon it again, this time with white flowers with a blotch of magenta at the base, in Kansu in 1913. A form similar to this latter was also found by Joseph Rock in the garden of a lamasery in the same area, and it is still grown under the name 'Joseph Rock'.

These tree paeonies are some of the finest small shrubs that grow in temperate gardens. The huge double flowers can reach thirty centimetres across, in all shades from white and pale pink to deep purple. They are easily grown, even on chalky soil, but can be damaged by late spring frosts, or mould encouraged by stagnant air.

Pæonia Moutan. Var. b.

appointed by the Queen, Marie-Amélie, to be Painter of flowers to Her Majesty; he was already giving lessons to the young princesses. The elder of the two daughters, Princess Louise-Marie, who was considered to be a talented artist, married Leopold I, the first King of the Belgians, in 1832, and before departing for her new country, presented Redouté with one of her flower paintings; in 1836, Redouté repaid the compliment by dedicating to her his *Choix de soixante roses*, described by him as "new, and not previously described." It was also almost certainly due partly to the Queen's respect for her old teacher that Redouté was awarded the title of "Chevalier of the Order of Leopold", for distinguished service to the Kingdom of Belgium (this was not the only public recognition of Redouté's talent; some years before, Charles X had made him a Chevalier de la Legion d'Honneur of France, a great distinction).

Between 1829 and 1837 publication of the *Histoire des Plantes Grasses*, on which work had stopped years earlier due to a quarrel between the botanist, de Candolle, and the publisher, M. Garnery, was resumed, with text by a different botanist, J.B. Antoine Guillemin, who also provided some of the text for the *Choix*. Projects such as this, and a number of less scientific, but aesthetically pleasing works, for example the *Collection de jolies petites fleurs*, published in 1835 with forty-eight plates, helped to ensure that Redouté's name did not slip entirely from public notice.

Redouté's latter years were beset by money worries, and he was forced to sell some of his furniture, silver and paintings, but he continued to paint and give lessons as busily as ever almost up to his death; the *Histoire . . . de Mais* by M. Bonafous, published in 1836, contains Redouté's last scientific drawing.

Rosa × damascena Celsiana

The damask rose is unknown in the wild, and its origins are obscure; it is thought by some to be a hybrid of the musk rose, *R. moschata*, and *R. gallica*. It has been in cultivation in Europe since the early sixteenth century, and may have been introduced into England from Italy by Dr Linaker, physician to Henry VII and Henry VIII; the "common and lesser damask roses" were listed by John Gerard in his famous book *The Herball or General Historie of Plants*, published in 1597, and Tradescant, in his catalogue of 1656, lists *R. damascena* as growing in his garden at Lambeth. In addition to its beautiful flowers, *R. damascena* was esteemed for its wonderful scent, and was used to make rose-water, while physicians were apparently more interested in the purgative liquor which could be obtained from it.

'Celsiana' is a graceful form of the damask, with lovely flowers which open an attractive shade of light pink, fading later. Presumably, it was named after M. Cels, whose fine garden in Paris is commemorated in the *Choix des Plantes donc la plupart sont cultivées dans le Jardin de Cels*, with text by Ventenat and illustrated by Redouté, and published in 1803.

Rosa Damascena.   *Rosier de Cels.*

P. J. Redouté pinx.   Imprimerie de Rémond   Charlin sculp.

Redouté died on June 20, 1840 while painting a lily brought to him by his daughter Joséphine; he was eighty-one. He had just received a letter from the Minister of the Interior, reneging on a verbal undertaking to purchase what was to have been an enormous and ambitious oil painting entitled the "Triomphe de Flora", started years before as a co-operative effort by Redouté and three friends, Percier, an architect, Thibault, and Gerard the portraitist. Whether or not the disappointment caused by this humiliation contributed to his sudden death (probably from a cerebral haemorrhage) or not, we shall never know. He was fortunate in his devoted wife and daughter, and his easy, generous nature ensured that he had numerous friends, and his funeral was attended by both eminent and ordinary people from all walks of life.

Although he had certainly been lucky in the patronage he had received over the years, he had also helped many less fortunate than himself. Perhaps the most fitting epitaph to his work were the prophetic words written years earlier by his friend and patron, L'Héritier: "Dear Redouté, the truth of your brush, even more than its magic, will make me share, perhaps, the celebrity that our work together will one day earn for us both."

Rosa pumila Jacq. *Rosier d'Amour*

Rosa pumila is now considered to be a form of *Rosa gallica* L. Botanically, the epithet *pumila* simply means 'dwarf', and this is an appropriate name for *Rosa gallica* which, in its wild form, is a low suckering shrub, with stems up to three feet high. The flowers themselves, however, are not notably smaller than usual, being around three inches across. This low-growing rose can be seen in the collection of old roses at Mottisfont Abbey in Hampshire, and is found as a wild plant from France and Germany southwards to the Caucasus, Turkey and Iraq, usually growing in rather dry, sandy soils.

It is the forerunner of the whole race of gallica roses, ranging from the old Apothecaries rose, or Rose of Provins (said to have been brought to Europe from the east by Thibaut IV, king of Navarre and Count of Champagne, who led the Crusade in 1239–1240), to the luscious roses of the late nineteenth century, such as 'Charles de Mills', with its very double, flat flowers of a deep reddish-purple, and heavy scent.

Rosa Pumila.   *Rosier d'Amour.*

P. J. Redouté pinx.   Imprimerie de Rémond   Beßin sculp.

Rosa gallica L. 'La Duchesse d'Orleans'

Rosa gallica is one of the best-loved of roses, known and cultivated since at least the twelfth century; numerous forms have been raised over the centuries since. The variety figured here does not appear to be in cultivation now, and little is known of its history, but it is probable that it was named after the Duchesse d'Orléans, later Her Majesty Queen Marie-Amelie, wife of Louis-Philippe I, to whom Redouté was appointed Painter of Flowers, and whose two daughters, Louise and Adelaide, were Redouté's pupils.

Monsieur Jacques, head gardener to the Duc d'Orléans at Château Neuilly from 1824–1832, raised three *Rosa sempervirens* hybrids, two of which were named after the two young princesses (the third was the well-known 'Felicite Perpetue'), and may well have raised this rose also. Redouté was obviously pleased with this likeness, as he later selected it for inclusion in the *Choix des plus belles fleurs*; it was first illustrated by him in *Les Roses*, and was described in the accompanying text by Thory as "one of the most beautiful of the group known as *Rosiers de France*".

Rosa Gallica Aurelianensis.

La Duchesse d'Orléans

P. J. Redouté.

Langlois.

Rosa × alba Regalis L. 'Great Maidens Blush'

This beautiful old shrub rose has been known to gardeners since the sixteenth century, or even earlier. It has many fanciful common names, amongst them 'Cuisse de Nymphe' and the well-known 'La Séduisante', and its free-flowering habit has ensured its continued popularity. It is one of the larger shrub roses, making strong growth up to about six feet tall with arching branches carrying the rather greyish foliage. The sweetly-scented blooms are borne from mid-June to early-July, and are a rather soft blush-pink at first, fading to pale creamy-pink at the edges, but retaining the pink colour at the centre of the flower.

Rosa alba Regalis.

Rosier blanc Royal.

P. J. Redouté pinx.

Imprimerie de Rémond.

Bessin sculp.

The North American Sylva. A description of the forest trees of the United States, Canada and Nova Scotia . . . by François André Michaux, translated from the French *Histoire des Arbres Forestiers de l'Amérique Septentrionale*, by A.L. Hillhouse was published in three volumes, between 1810 and 1813, as a quarto with 140 coloured stipple engravings by Redouté and his pupil, Bessa; the English translation was published in Philadelphia in 1818–1819. Michaux had lived with his father, André Michaux, in America for ten years, and this book was published as a record of their time as plant collectors and nurserymen in eastern North America.

Quercus macrocarpa Michx.

This deciduous oak, which was introduced into cultivation in 1811, was first described by Michaux in 1801. It makes a large tree, growing up to 170 feet high in the wild, and has grey, flaky bark. The unusual acorn cup, in which the scales near the rim form a kind of mossy fringe, has led to it being known as the 'burr oak' or 'mossy-cup oak'. *Quercus macrocarpa* grows on rich soil from Nova Scotia to Manitoba, Wyoming, Massachusetts, Georgia, Kansas and Texas.

1

Quercus palustris MUENCHH.

The pin oak, or swamp oak, as it is sometimes known, enjoys moist conditions, and is found from Massachusetts to Michigan, Virginia and Arkansas; it was introduced to England in 1800, and flourishes here as a quick-growing, but rather short-lived tree. It is deciduous, and can grow up to one hundred feet high; when conditions are favourable the leaves turn a deep scarlet in the autumn. Like those of many American oaks, the acorns of *Quercus palustris* take two seasons to mature.

ALBUM DE REDOUTÉ. The *Album de Redouté*, dedicated to the Duchesse de Berry, a friend and patron of Redouté, and daughter-in-law of Charles X, was published by Bossange in Paris in 1824; it consists of twenty-nine colour engravings, taken from *Les Liliacées* and *Les Roses*, with a frontispiece.

Tulipa gesneriana L. *dracontia*

Tulipa gesneriana L., is the name applied to a large and variable group of tulips, which are all thought to be clones of the species which Linnaeus first described in his *Species Plantarum* in 1753. Its exact origins in the wild are obscure, although it probably came from Central Asia, and it is found naturalized on cultivated ground throughout south-western Europe. Since the sixteenth century, and possibly earlier in Turkey, the garden tulip was hybridized so much that it is now virtually impossible to distinguish the true characters of the species. The name *gesneriana* commemorates Conrad Gessner, a Swiss zoologist, who in his book *De Hortis Germaniae*, published in 1561, illustrated a tulip grown from Turkish seed; the varietal name *dracontia*, meaning 'dragon' refers to what we now call parrot tulips, but seems a more appropriate description for this fierce-looking flower.

Tulipa Gesneriana.

Var. Dracontia.

P. J. Redouté pinx.

Tulipe des Jardins.

Var. le Dragon.

Langlois sculp.

CHOIX DES PLUS BELLES FLEURS. *Choix des plus belles fleurs, prises dans différentes familles du règne végétal et de quelques branches des plus beaux fruits, souvent animées par des insectes*, was published as a folio in Paris from 1827–1833. All 144 plates, selected for their beauty rather than for any scientific purpose, were drawn by Redouté, and engraved by Bessin, Chapuy, Langlois and Victor. Each plate was colour printed and hand finished with watercolour.

Bouquet de Pensées

La pensée conveys the double meaning of thoughts and flowers. Pansies and the closely related violets, were very popular in both France and England during the early nineteenth century, and it is perhaps interesting to note that Napoleon adopted the violet as his symbol (it is hard to imagine a more incongruous choice), in contrast to the white lily traditionally favoured by the French monarchy. In addition to being prized for their delicate scent and sentimental associations, violets and pansies were a source of scientific interest to those, such as Charles Darwin, who were beginning to question the concept of the immutable nature of species. By studying 'improved varieties of the Heartsease', Darwin was able to add weight to his theories by noting the rapidity of the changes of colour and markings which were being obtained by breeding. The pansies illustrated here are garden types which are derived from crossing *Viola tricolor*, the heartsease native to Europe and western Asia, with *Viola lutea* and possibly *Viola altaica*, from Central Asia.

Bouquet de Pensées.

Camellia blanc

'Alba Simplex' is a variety of *Camellia japonica* L., a native of Japan and Korea, but long cultivated in China. Camellias of all types have been popular with gardeners since they were first introduced into Europe at the beginning of the eighteenth century, and although they were at first thought to require greenhouse protection it was later discovered that the majority of them could tolerate the English climate, provided that they were given sufficient shelter from cold winds. Due to its doubtful hardiness, the camellia became popular as a conservatory plant during the nineteenth century, and in Redouté's time it was grown in a tub as a plant for the orangery.

In the wild, *Camellia japonica* has red flowers, but as it freely produces mutant branches it has given rise to many different varieties. By the nineteenth century there were around a thousand forms, with single, double or semi-double flowers in shades of red, pink and white, and a bewildering array of markings.

At the time the *Choix des plus belles fleurs* was published, 'Alba Simplex' would have been something of a novelty, as it was raised only in 1813, at the Tooting Nursery, London. It was first recorded in 1819 by Samuel Curtis under the name 'flore albo simplici', and in 1822 it was illustrated in Loddiges' *Botanical Cabinet*.

Camellia blanc.   *Camellia Japonica.*

P. J. Redouté.   Bessin.

Pois de senteur

The sweet pea, *Lathyrus odoratus* L., originates from Sicily and southern Italy, where it grows on rough ground and rocky hills. It has been cultivated in English gardens since 1699, when seeds were sent by Father Cupani of Italy to Dr Uvedale at Enfield, and has been a popular plant ever since; it was described by William Robinson in *The English Flower Garden* (1883) as "Perhaps the most precious annual plant grown".

The breeding of sweet peas, which led to the many large-flowered garden varieties available today, was started in the 1870's by Henry Eckford, a nurseryman from Shropshire, and in 1900 the variety 'Prima Donna', with wavy standards, gave rise to a new strain of 'Spencer' sweet peas, so-called because one of the first of them was named after Countess Spencer. From then on new varieties were raised in vast numbers, with every kind of colour and flower form represented (sometimes at the expense of the gorgeous scent), and breeding continues today.

Pois de senteur.

Lathyrus odoratus.

P. J. Redouté.

Langlois.

Noisetier franc à gros fruits

The hazel, *Corylus avellana* L., is a native of Europe, including most parts of the British Isles, western Asia, and parts of North Africa, and it has been esteemed for many years both as a source of food, and for its quick-growing stems, which when coppiced are used for hurdle-fencing and as pea and bean sticks. The ancient Greeks and Romans mentioned hazels in their writings, and referred to their supposed magic properties, and hazel twigs are today still regarded as particularly efficacious by water diviners. *Corylus maxima* Mill., the cob nut, illustrated here, comes from northern Turkey, and is grown commercially in Kent, while the Abbé Coste, in his *Flore Descriptive et Illustrée de la France, de la Corse et des contrées limitrophes*, published in 1910, describes a variety, *Corylus grandis* Dryand., which is 'remarquable par ses gros fruits qu'on livre au commerce.' Other varieties have been raised over the years, usually for their fruits, but hazels are also valuable for their ornamental catkins, which are at their most attractive in about February, a time of year when interesting shrubs for the garden are in short supply. Due to its very pliable branches, the hazel was used in the pleached allées favoured in formal French gardens, and this may be one reason why Redouté selected it for inclusion in this book.

Noisetier franc à gros fruits. . . . *Corylus maxima.*

Oeillet panaché

The name of the carnation, *Dianthus caryophyllus* L., is derived from the Greek diosanthos (heavenly flower) and karuophullon (referring to the dried flowers of the clove tree), an apt description of the wonderful spicy scent which emanates from the flowers. It is found either wild or naturalized throughout the Mediterranean, and was introduced into England at some stage, possibly by the Normans; Gerard mentions the 'Clove Gillofloure' in his *Herball* (1597) and John Tradescant lists 'severall sorts of great dainty Gilliflowers or Carnations' as well as single and double carnations in the catalogue of his museum at South Lambeth, published in 1656. Interestingly, in view of Redouté's association with the Empress Joséphine at Malmaison, there is a whole group of greenhouse carnations known as 'Malmaisons', with stiff stems and spectacularly large double flowers. There seems to have been no direct connection with the garden at Malmaison, Joséphine having died years earlier, but a blush-coloured seedling, 'Souvenir de Malmaison' was raised in France in 1857, and is supposed to have been called this because of its likeness to the rose of the same name, which had been raised in 1842, and was, incidentally, illustrated by Redouté in the *Choix des Plus Belles Roses*.

Œillet panaché.

Dianthus cariophyllus.

P. J. Redouté.

Chapuy.

Oreilles d'Ours

Auriculas *Primula x pubescens* Jacq., have been cultivated in Europe for over four hundred years, and whilst no-one can be certain of its origins, it appears that the cultivated auricula is derived from *Primula x pubescens*, itself a natural hybrid between *P. auricula* and *P. hirsuta*, two species from the European Alps. As early as 1544 an Italian botanist, Mattioli, described and illustrated the auricula, and his contemporary, Clusius, described a plant with red whitish-centred flowers as *Auricula ursi* II (bears ears). Auriculas were probably introduced into England towards the end of the sixteenth century, and by 1596, Gerard was able to describe various types of auriculas in his *Herball*. Tradescant, in his catalogue of 1656, lists fourteen different forms of 'Auricula ursi', including 'striped white and red Bears eares', 'party coloured white and purple Bears eares' and, finally, but rather vaguely, 'several sorts of bears ears'. There has long been a strong tradition of growing what were known as 'florist's flowers' (amongst them, auriculas, carnations and pinks) as a relief from the rigours of working life in the polluted industrial towns in the midlands and north of England, and this is partly due to the influx of Flemish weavers to the area in the eighteenth century. These refugees brought with them a knowledge and love of plants that led to the formation of florists societies, and in the 1870's a National Auricula Society was founded, which exists to this day.

Rosier de Bancks var. à fleurs jaunes

This yellow form of the Banksian rose, *Rosa banksiae* R. Brown 'Lutea', was introduced for the Horticultural Society (now the Royal Horticultural Society) by John Parks, who brought back a number of plants from Kiangsu, China in 1824. The white form, known as *Rosa banksiae* 'Banksiae' or 'Alba Plena', had been introduced to England by William Kerr, who collected for Kew, in 1807, and described by Robert Brown in Aiton's *Hortus Kewensis*; the name is in honour of the wife of Sir Joseph Banks, the great botanist and explorer, at whose house in London Redouté made the acquaintance of many of the well-known botanists of his day.

The yellow form of *Rosa banksiae* is known only as a garden plant, and, chiefly because it is much less thorny than the wild plant, *Rosa banksiae* var. *normalis*, it may be a hybrid between that and a yellow china rose. It is also the hardiest and most free-flowering of the Banksian roses, although it has less scent than the others, and it can be grown outside only in mild parts of England, and the southern states of the U.S.A.

Rosier de Bancks var. *à fleurs jaunes*.

P. J. Redouté.

Bunch of flowers

This charming study, in pencil and watercolour on vellum, is in the possession of the Fitzwilliam Museum, Cambridge, to whom it was bequeathed by the second Lord Fairhaven as part of the Broughton collection. Amongst the flowers are asters, gentians, hibiscus, roses, and a tree paeony; the addition of the butterfly shows that Redouté's skill as a draughtsman was not limited to flowers, and, in fact, the title of the first edition of the *Choix des plus belles fleurs* states that it was "souvent animées par des insectes".

P. J. Redouté

A wreath of wild roses

This wreath forms the frontispiece of *Les Roses*, and shows a selection of wild roses including the yellow *Rosa foetida*, the Austrian briar. It is interesting that there is no bright red; the Chinese roses which have this colour, such as *Rosa moyesii*, were not brought to Europe until the early twentieth century.

The Greek ode in the middle of the wreath is by the poet Anacreon of Teos in Ionia, who migrated to Abdera in 540 B.C., but spent most of his life in Tsamos or Athens. His poems are small and graceful, often praising love or wine. This one was rendered rather freely by the Irish poet, Thomas Moore in around 1810:

> Buds of Roses, virgin flowers,
> Culled from Cupid's balmy bowers,
> In the bowl of Bacchus steep,
> Till in crimson drops they weep.
> Twine the rose, the garland twine,
> Every leaf distilling wine;
> Drink and smile, and learn to think
> That we were born to smile and drink.
> Rose thou art the sweetest flower
> That ever drank the amber shower.
> Rose, thou art the fondest child,
> Of dimpled spring, the wood-nymph wild.

A more literal, but pedestrian translation might be:

Put a garland on me, and I will play my lyre to you at Bacchus temple. I will dance with my buxom girl, fetchingly decked with a chaplet made of roses.

126

Στέφον δυ με και λυρίζω
Παρα τοις Διονυσα σηκοις,
Μετα Κδρης βαθυκολπω,
Ροδινοισι σεφανισκοις,
Πεπυκασμενος χορευσω.

Anacreon Ode V.

P. J. Redouté pinx.   Imprimerie de Rémond   Charlin sculp.

INDEX

SELECTED REFERENCES

Blunt, W. and Stearn, W.T. *The Art of Botanical Illustration* Collins 1950

Henrey, Blanche *British Botanical and Horticultural Literature before 1800* Oxford University Press 1975

Mallary, Peter and Francis A *Redouté Treasury* Dent 1986

Mathew, Brian et al. *P.J. Redouté: Lilies and Related Flowers* Michael Joseph 1982

Léger, Charles *Redouté et son temps* Paris 1945

Nissen, Claus *Die Botanische Buchillustration* Stuttgart 1951

Ridge, Antonia *The Man Who Painted Roses* Faber & Faber 1974

Rix, Martyn *The Art of the Botanist* Lutterworth 1981

Scrase, David *Flowers of Three Centuries* International Exhibition Foundation 1983–4

Stearn, William T. and Rix, Martyn *Redouté's Fairest Flowers* Herbert/BMNH 1987